Alchemy of Life

Reflections on Transformation & Becoming

Kayla M. Sweet

BookLeaf Publishing

India | USA | UK

To my love, my artist, my husband, my kindred spirit—

You have seen me in all my seasons, through the unraveling and the becoming. Your love has been both sanctuary and catalyst, steady as the earth beneath me and vast as the sky above. Thank you for believing in my voice, for holding space for my dreams, and for walking beside me as I continue to transform.

This book is a reflection of my journey, but you are woven into every word.

With all my love,

Kayla

Acknowledgement

No journey of transformation happens in isolation, and neither does the creation of a book. *Alchemy of Life* exists because of the love, support, and inspiration of so many, and I am endlessly grateful for each person who has touched my life along the way.

To my husband—my love, my muse, my steady ground. Your unwavering belief in me, your patience, and your ability to see the beauty in my becoming have been a gift beyond words. Thank you for holding space for my creativity, for the late-night conversations, and for reminding me of my own magic when I forget.

To my closest friends and kindred spirits—you know who you are. Thank you for walking this path with me, for witnessing my growth, and for reflecting my light back to me. Your encouragement, deep conversations, and reminders to rest have helped shape not only this book but also the person I am becoming.

To my mentors, teachers, and guides—whether in person or through the words of your books, the wisdom you have shared has been a lantern on my path. Your insights, your courage, and your willingness to tell the truth have given me permission to do the same.

To Miss Kitty—my wise and gentle companion, the soul wrapped in fur who teaches me so much about presence, resilience, and unconditional love. Thank you for spending the last 18 years by my side when I was becoming the woman I am today.

To the readers—to you. Thank you for picking up this book, for allowing my words to enter your heart, and for being on your own journey of becoming. Transformation is not always easy, but it is always worth it. If these pages resonate with you, inspire you, or simply remind you that you are not alone, then this book has fulfilled its purpose.

And finally, to the past versions of myself—the ones who doubted, who struggled, who searched, and who dared to hope. You made this possible. You walked through the fire so I could stand here, with words to share and a heart open to the infinite possibilities ahead.

Preface

Transformation is not a destination. It is a daily invitation. A quiet becoming. A lifelong unfolding. It lives in the sacred ordinary, in the breath between thoughts, in the ache of memory, in the glimmer of hope after a long season of pain.

This collection began as a month-long practice, a devotional rhythm of reflection, presence, and poetry. Each day of March 2025, I wrote from the pulse of now, from the light in my afternoon walks, the grief in my chest, the joy that caught me off guard. But as the writing continued, I found myself immersed in deep waters.

What began as a practice of daily noticing became an excavation. A healing. An honoring. A remembering. Many of these poems were born in March and early April of 2025. But others, perhaps some of the most tender, raw, and aching, were written years ago, in seasons of heartbreak, loss, or quiet transformation. I include them here not to dwell in the past, but to give voice to it. To show you the whole truth, not just where I am, but where I've been.

These poems are not arranged chronologically. They are woven like memory: fluid, spiraling, nonlinear. They will take you forward and backward through time, through the echoes of my mind, and through the many lives I've lived within this one.

Some are gentle. Some are heavy. Some shimmer with hope. Some bleed with honesty. But all of them are true. All of them are alive. This collection is a testament to the quiet power of alchemy, the art of turning pain into wisdom, grief into gold, and ordinary life into something sacred.

It's for the seekers. The feelers. The ones standing at the edge of a new beginning, or sitting in the soft ruins of something lost. It's for anyone who's ever wondered if their small moments mattered.

They do. They always have.

May these words meet you exactly where you are. May they whisper the truth that healing is not linear, and becoming never ends. May you feel seen. May you feel less alone. And may you remember: the alchemy of life is already happening within and around you.

With love and deep reverence for your path,
Kayla

March Again

It's March again,
and the spring air and raindrops tease me.
Winter didn't stretch as long this year
not as cold, not as slow,
not as heavy in my bones.

Maybe it was never winter's fault
that the frost seeped into my soul.
Because the cold still came,
and the snow still fell,
but I stayed warm
alive.

Maybe the seasons don't shape us
as much as we shape them,

our aches and longings
etched onto the weather,
naming the wind,
calling it ours.

The Body Remembers

Sometimes, I still forget to breathe,
though my mind knows better.
My body remembers the days
when breath was hard-won
trembling, uneasy.

But when I do breathe,
it washes over me like an ocean wave,
cleansing, softening,
reminding me:
Nothing here asks me to hold my breath.

I have come so far
from where I once stood.
My feet no longer ache
from the journey that carried me here,
but my heart still remembers
every step.

Homecoming

Coming home
isn't a return to before,
nor an anchor to a place
or time.

Coming home
is hearing your own voice,
feeling your own emotions,
breathing your own breath
and knowing, deeply,
what it means to be you
from the inside out.

I come home to myself
again and again,
and in each homecoming,
I gather pieces of myself
I once left behind
fragments of truth,
whispers of longing,
the quiet knowing
of what has always mattered.

Home in Him

When he's with me,
I am home.

I never knew safety
could be something I felt
in the quiet presence of another
a warmth deeper than skin,
a stillness that settles the soul.

He awoke that in me.

Showed me what it means
to be seen,
known,
loved
not for what I could be,
not for what I give,
but simply for existing.

I never knew the weightlessness
of being fully accepted,
cherished,
desired
until him.

And now, I wake
to the scent of him woven into morning,
breathe him in like something holy.
His warmth reaches me
before his hands do,
before his voice does,
before I even open my eyes.

And when he looks at me,
like I am everything

I believe him.
And maybe, for the first time,
I believe in love
the way love always
believed in me.

This Is How Alive Feels

This is how alive feels
wind tangling in my hair,
sun kissing my skin,
cool grass grounding me,
bare feet pressing into the earth
like I belong here.

Heart open,
heart broken,
heart overflowing
all at once.

A skipped beat.
A quickened breath.
I feel it all.

Gratitude pulses through my veins
like medicine,
while fear whispers its old familiar script.
Love spills over,
a river fed by the thaw of winter,
wild and relentless,
rushing toward everything
it was meant to reach.

And still, my heart aches
for every soul
who woke up in pain today.

It's a complicated thing
to hold the weight of so many blessings
in the same hands
that cradle grief,
anger,
fear.

But I do.

I let it all wash over me,
like summer rain
unexpected, cleansing, whole.

I invite these emotions in,
set the table,
pour the tea,
listen as they speak in the only languages they
know.

I hold the contradictions,
the tangled truths,
the paradox of it all

because this is how alive feels.

Hello, Soul

Hello, Soul
I've been waiting.
Waiting to pick up the thread
of this long-overdue conversation,
this quiet, creative collaboration
between the deepest parts of me.

I feel the cracks in my skin,
the places where I once held too tightly,
softening now,
letting you out,
letting me in.

You move with the breeze,
whispering songs into my heart,
melodies woven from all that lights me up.

I hear the echoes of your wisdom
humming beneath my skin,
steady, certain,
like something ancient
I am just now remembering.

I accept your invitation
to reflect, to pause, to listen.
But maybe, most of all,
I accept the invitation to play.

To chase the wind.
To color outside the lines.
To dance in the spaces
where wonder lives.

To be alive
not just in thought,
but in laughter, in untamed movement,
in the wild, unfiltered joy
of simply being.

The Weight We Carry

Everyone here carries weight
silent burdens, buried strengths,
a carefully curated image
that shows only pieces of the whole.

Seeking approval.
Seeking love.
Seeking validation.

If only they knew
what I know
that they were never meant
to carry so much.

The weight was never theirs to hold.

If only they knew
they could release it,
excavate the gifts within,
unearth the wisdom
that has always been there,
waiting.

But they forgot.
Forgot how to listen
when the world is silent.

Forgot how to hear
the deep well of knowing
that speaks beneath the noise.

And so I wonder
How do you teach someone
to remember themselves?
To trust the quiet?

To find their way back
to the truth that was never lost,
only buried?

Focus Me

My mind is wild horses
delicate glass in motion.
I don't want to break them.

They carry me away,
quickly, fiercely,
thrilling and untamed.
Exciting.
Distracting.

But sometimes, they take me
too far,
too fast,
away from where I need to be.

And the medicine the doctor gave me
to train them, tame them
makes me sick.

How do I find my way?
How do I guide them,
not with reins,
but with trust?

What if it isn't control I'm after,
but clarity
not breaking,
but refining?

What if riding the wild horses
into the night
into stars,
dreams,
open skies
isn't about restraint,
but focus?

Not a cage,
but a sharpening.

Like turning the lens of a camera,
birthing clarity
from the blurry shapes
of what could be.

Sharpen.
Tune.
Focus me.

Who Am I Today?

Who am I
today?

Not the same as yesterday,
or last week,
or last year,
or even five breaths ago.

I am born new
with each moment
a breath of fresh air,
an unfolding,
an adventure,
an opportunity.

Who am I?

I am a soul
swimming in eternity.
A lover,
tenderly embracing each fleeting moment.
A detective,
curiously gathering clues
about who I am today
what I need,
what nourishes me,
what calls me forward.

Who am I?

I am a cosmic adventurer,
seeking connection,
pulling at the golden threads
that weave us together.

I follow the red threads of belonging,
of love,
of destiny,
tying me to you,

tying me to myself,
leading me home
again and again.

Who am I today?

Open.
Curious.
New.

And who will I be tomorrow?

I won't know
until I meet her.

Craving Depth

Sometimes, in a crowd,
I feel the loneliest of all.

The echoes of small talk blur around me
weather,
yes, the sun is shining.
Busyness,
all the things filling schedules.
New cars,
new houses,
mile markers of lives moving forward.

Everyone is reaching,
trying to connect,
but I get lost in the hum of it all,
spinning, dizzy,
with nowhere to fall.

I smile. I nod.
But inside, I am wondering

What makes you feel alive?
What was your greatest heartbreak?
What is life teaching you, right now,
in the quiet spaces
between words?

I crave depth.

To see the soul beneath the surface,
to hear the truth
beneath the practiced lines,
to feel the texture of unspoken emotions
woven behind the persona.

But social conditioning
has taught me to swallow my curiosities,

to keep them folded inside my chest
like love letters
never sent.

So I stay quiet.
I listen
not just to the words,
but to the pauses,
the hesitations,
the weight behind them.

And I dream of the day
when my questions will no longer
be too much.

When my words
will open doors,
unravel souls,
and forge the kind of connection
that feels like home.

Living With Cats: A Love Story (and a Hostage Situation)

When you live with cats,
you wake up to things crashing.
Not just small things
big things.
Glass shattering, plants toppling,
the unmistakable sound of regret.

At 3 AM, they reenact gladiator battles.
At 6 AM, they scream like they're dying.
(They are not dying.
They are just…
slightly hungry.)

When you live with cats,
nothing you own is really yours.
The couch? Theirs.
The bed? Theirs.
Your laptop? A heated throne.
Your dignity? Gone.

The walls are as scratched up as the furniture.
Your legs bear the scars of unsolicited
ambushes.
You think you're in charge,
but they have already claimed your soul.

They decide when it's playtime.
They decide when it's nap time.
They decide when it's time
to sprint across the house
like they just remembered
a grudge from 2017.

But then
when you least expect it
they choose you.

A headbutt to the face.
A slow blink from across the room.
A gentle paw resting on your chest.
A purr so deep it could recalibrate your
nervous system.

You realize
you have become their favorite nap spot,
their warmest place in the world.

When you live with cats,
you earn their love,
and when they pick you for cuddles,
you feel like a goddess,
chosen, anointed, blessed.

They will make you laugh
fall off furniture with zero shame,
chase ghosts that do not exist,
steal your food,

reject the expensive toys you bought
in favor of a crumpled receipt.

They heal you with reiki purring when you're
sick.
They stare into the void at 2 AM to keep the
demons away.
They demand attention,
and somehow,
you find yourself giving it gladly.

Because they look at you
like you are some kind of wonderful,
like you are worthy of devotion,
like they knew you
in another lifetime.

And they teach you
the beauty of doing whatever you please,
the power of resting with ease,
the art of not giving a single thought
to what anyone else thinks.

Living with cats is an honor,
an adventure,
a privilege,
a built-in alarm clock
that does not come with a snooze button.

And a friendship
like no other.

It's All a Dream

It's all a dream
the big things,
the little things,
the endless preoccupations
we weave into meaning.

Colors, textures, stories,
emotions so vast
they could split the sky.

It's all a dream
a beautiful, terrible,

exhilarating illusion,
a construction of our lives
so convincing,
we forget
we built it ourselves.

Was it a good dream?
A bad dream?

I have a fondness
for the ones that wake me
drenched in sweat,
pulse racing,
lungs grasping for breath.

Those are the interesting ones.
The ones that shake loose the illusions,
the ones that demand
we decode the mystery.

Because who can really tell
if we are awake or asleep?

It's all a dream
vivid, simmering, unraveling,

stories looping, rewriting,
shaping who we are,
who we could be.

Heroes, villains, victims
they all exist here,
changing roles,
shifting shapes,
no one staying the same
for long.

How do you dream?

Are you lucid,
taking hold of the narrative,
bending reality to your will?

Or are you floating,
swept into the tide,
letting the dream dream you?

Either way,
it's a lovely dream.

So tell me
when you wake,
will you remember?

Take a Walk With Me

Take a walk with me.

Let's step outside
and invite the sun
to slip into our bones,
to warm the spaces
we forgot needed light.

Let's let the wind
steal our worries,
tangle itself in our hair,
whisper something ancient
as it moves through the trees.

Let's listen
to birds singing secrets,
to children's laughter
echoing like little bells,
to the hum of a world
alive with its own rhythm.

Let's make our feet
familiar with the roads
that have always been near
but never truly seen.

Let's see the world
with childlike eyes
wide open,
curious,
soft enough for wonder,
brave enough for adventure.

Let's make friends
with the passing cars,
the rustling leaves,
the quiet conversations
of neighbors trimming their hedges,

sweeping their porches,
living their lives.

Take a walk with me,
and let's find something
we thought we left behind.

Let's let our souls
be the compass.
No phones,
no maps
just curiosity.

Let's let the colors of the grass,
the cracks in the pavement,
the scattered stones
paint our imaginations
with untold stories
and unseen possibilities.

Take a walk with me
not just down the street,
but into the infinite,
into the spaces
where time dissolves,

where presence is everything,
where we remember
we were always free.

To Love You Through

What an honor it is
to stand by your side
as you slowly, softly
fade from this world.

To hold space
for your thinning body,
your trembling muscles,
your delicate, shaking bones
for those weary,
yet endlessly loving eyes.

Today is fluids day
the day I've learned to love,

even as it breaks my heart.
A ritual of hope,
of comfort,
of one more borrowed moment
together.

This simple bag of life,
clear and quiet,
has held you here
nourishing you
longer than we ever imagined.
So many bonus days,
bonus weeks,
bonus months
since I first heard
you were transitioning
to the other side.

I never knew
my heart could stretch
this wide
to hold so much
love,
grief,
pain,

and gratitude
all at once.

At first, the pain was unbearable.
I couldn't imagine
a world without you.
I still can't.

But in the months
since I found out you were leaving,
something has shifted in me.

You've taught me
to see the beauty
in everything
even dying.
Especially dying.

You've shown me
strength in stillness,
resilience in fragility,
a fierce love for life
woven into every quiet breath.

You've soothed my soul
with your soft purrs,
your gentle glances
reassuring me:
you are not suffering.
You are simply fading,
gently,
gracefully.

Sustained by love
and lactated Ringer's solution.
Held by tenderness.
Carried by presence.

You've taught me
we can meet even fate
with open arms.
That the small, soft moments
the ones the world might overlook
are the ones
we'll carry
forever.

I'll never be ready
to say goodbye.

But somehow,
I know you'll make
even that
beautiful.

And I'll be here
loving you through it all.
Loving you
into the light.

Thank you,
my beloved.
For every sacred second.
For letting me walk this path
with you.

The Sacred Pause

Some days,
my heart feels tender.
My soul grows quiet.
And tiredness
envelopes me
like a soft, gray fog.

Some days,
I have to stop
a screeching halt
in the middle of my momentum
and do nothing.

Because the days of going,
moving,
doing,
producing,
achieving
feel exhilarating...
until they don't.

And my body
says no
not with words,
but with silence
that echoes louder
than any alarm.

Going.
Going.
Going.

STOP!

I drop.
I surrender.
I sink into stillness
a quiet moment,
soft and slow.

I catch my breath.
I feel the ache
of the parts within me
that move at different speeds.

One part
craves acceleration
it loves to build, to create,
to dance in the thrill
of motion.

Another part
dreams of simpler things:
a porch swing,
an open sky,
a quiet morning
with no expectations.

And I
I am all of it.

The ambition and the ache.
The movement and the rest.
The fire and the fading light.

Tiredness washes over me
like a teacher.

I've learned to stop
and listen
to the whispers
of simplicity,
to the hush
beneath the hustle.

To let stillness speak.
To choose intention
over inertia.
To remember
that momentum
is not the same
as meaning.

When I Remember to Breathe

I breathe in
deep,
slow,
like the tide returning home.

The air washes over me
like waves
kissing the shore,
gentle and eternal.

I breathe out
a soft sigh,
my whole body

whispering goodbye
to thoughts,
to stories,
to identities
that are no longer mine.

I close my eyes
and feel the quiet hum
of energy
pulsing through me
behind my eyes,
beneath my feet,
in the steady rhythm
of my beating heart.

A rhythm I can sway to.
A rhythm that reminds me
I'm still here.

I connect to myself.
I connect to you.
I become the air
in the room
invisible, essential,
Everywhere.

I root into the floor beneath me,
anchor into the moment,
and I feel both
here and not here,
free and not free,
body and spirit
woven together
in stillness.

I breathe.

I fill myself
with sweet nourishment
always available,
so often forgotten.

And as I exhale,
my shoulders drop.
The tension lifts.
The weight of old versions of me
falls away.

I let go
of the things
I thought I was
before I remembered
to breathe.

Lead Consciously

How do we lead
consciously?

With presence.
With intentionality.
With self-awareness
woven into the fabric
of every decision,
every breath.

This question isn't just the one I ask others
it's the one I return to again and again
within myself.

Because for me,
conscious leadership
isn't about control
or being perfect.

It's about presence.
It's about choosing again.
It's about being honest enough
to pause
and ask:
Am I aligned?
Am I listening?

To lead consciously,
I've learned
I must first be willing to feel.

To slow down
when everything around me
says speed up.

To stay with discomfort
long enough
to learn from it.

To tell myself the truth
not the polished version,
not the shoulds,
not the story I wish were true
but the actual truth.

To see what is
instead of what I hoped,
pretended,
or was taught to believe.

I've had to drop old narratives
about what leadership should look like,
about who I need to be
to be taken seriously,
about worthiness
and proving.

I've had to get quiet
to hear what matters.
And sometimes,
the truth that rises
is not what I expect.

Sometimes it's inconvenient,
or humbling,
or holy.

But always,
it brings me home.

Home to myself.
Home to integrity.
Home to love.

When I lead from that place
from my grounded,
imperfect,
heart-centered self
something sacred happens.

I stop trying to be something
other than me. .
I start connecting.
I let go of needing to know
and lean into curiosity.

I choose to create,
to receive,

to play,
to rest,
to trust
the quiet nudges of my soul
over the loud demands of the world.

This path
asks a lot of me.

It asks for courage
to be seen,
to be questioned,
to sometimes get it wrong
and begin again
with grace.

It asks for humility
to listen before speaking,
to learn from others,
to admit when I've missed the mark.

It asks for softness
a kind of fierce tenderness
that can hold both boundaries
and compassion.

But this path
this conscious, soul-led way
gives back even more.

It gives me clarity
about who I am
and what I value.

It gives me relationships
that are rooted in truth.

It gives me freedom
to lead without losing myself,
to honor both my voice
and the voices of others.

And it reminds me
that leadership is not a role I play,
but a reflection
of how I live,
how I love,
and how I show up
in the small, unseen moments.

This is how I lead.
Consciously.
Lovingly.
With presence.

Not perfectly
but fully,
and on purpose

I Still Tremble

My hands still tremble
every time I speak
in front of a crowd.

My voice still shakes
subtly, maybe so subtly
no one else would notice.

But I notice.

Cheeks hot,
Mouth dry.

Remnants remain
echoes of the girl

who was once too terrified
to share her voice.

The pressure I placed on myself
to be perfect
used to strangle my breath,
tighten my chest,
turn my vision white.

I once fainted
in the hallway after
just trying to speak.

That girl
that version of me
still lives in my memory,
but she doesn't scare me anymore.

Now, when the nerves come,
I greet them like old friends.
I notice the shaking,
and I know
my body is simply preparing me
to share something sacred.

Something true.
Something only I can say
in the way I was meant to say it.

This isn't about perfection.
This is about connection.

Yes
my heart still races,
my breath still catches,
but I remember:

Fear and excitement
wear the same skin.
So I choose excitement.
I choose fire.
I choose life.

I choose to share the stories,
the lessons,
the messages
that once saved me
because I know
they might just save someone else, too.

I choose to speak,
even when I shake.

Because the truth is
I was born to do this.
Even if my soul prefers
the quiet intimacy
of one-on-one conversation,
there is something holy
about standing before many
and letting my heart be seen.

So I take a deep, shaky breath.
I sigh it out.
I let the nervous laugh escape.
I smile
genuinely,
not to perform,
but to remember I'm alive.

And then I look out at the crowd.

Not just at faces,
but at souls.

Each one carrying
a story
waiting to be heard,
a life
waiting to be honored.

And in that moment,
I don't try to be perfect.
I don't try to impress.

I simply
Connect.

Promises of Spring

My garden
looks like a wasteland
a forgotten corner of beauty
after a long, neglectful winter.

What once bloomed
only months ago
now lies crumpled and gray,
petals turned to ash,
life paused
beneath broken branches,
and half-finished dreams
left behind
by the cold.

Everywhere I turn,
evidence of interruption.
Projects halted.
Plans abandoned.
Roots holding on in silence.

From a distance,
everything looks dead.
Dry.
Unloved.

But I step in closer.

This is the garden
my husband and I planted
a sacred space
to celebrate our love story,
our shared soil.

And as I walk its winding paths,
survey the damage,
and whisper apologies
to the land I left untended,
I begin again
with my hands,

my eyes,
my heart.

I kneel beside
each seemingly lifeless plant
and look closely
past the brittle stems,
beneath the matted leaves
of last fall's sorrow.

And there
hidden in the mess,
sheltered beneath decay
tiny signs of life.

Buds, barely visible,
green and urgent.
Resilient shoots
pushing up from the base
of what I thought
was long gone.

The garden isn't dead.
It's preparing.
Becoming.

Holding the quiet
promises of spring.

And as I brush the soil
from my fingertips
and feel that familiar
flutter in my chest,
I realize

those promises of spring
also live in me.

Even in the seasons
when I feel dry,
gray,
Forgotten
something tender
is always growing
beneath the surface.

The sacred
always
survives
the cold.

Talk to Me About the Real Things

Small talk makes me tired.
But real conversation
the kind that cuts through the noise
fuels my soul.

Deeper-level connection
lights me up from the inside,
propels me forward
with a force so strong,
I sometimes don't realize
how moved I've been
until afterward.

So please
don't talk to me about the weather,
or which team won last night's game.

Talk to me about
the meaning of life.
Tell me about your biggest heartbreak,
the moment you thought
you couldn't go on
and how you found your way
back to yourself.

Tell me about the things
that make your eyes glow,
that spark your curiosity,
that keep you up at night
because they matter too much to ignore.

Tell me about the supernatural moment
you never shared with anyone
because even you
wouldn't have believed it
if it hadn't happened to you.

Talk to me about synchronicities,
gut feelings,
and the magic that doesn't make sense
but somehow feels more real
than anything else.

Talk to me about grief,
about what you had to release
to become who you are now.

Tell me when you've felt
most in love,
or in luck,
or in lust
and what those moments taught you
about being alive.

Tell me about the contradictions
you carry
the competing parts inside you,
each with its own voice,
its own longing,
its own dream.

Tell me about your childhood,
your family,
the quiet ache you've never named.

Tell me the things
you've buried deep
the truths you hide,
hoping to forget,
but never really do.

Talk to me about these things
and let me love all of you.

And if you bare your soul to me,
I'll show you mine.

I'll tell you about my scars,
and how I've turned them into gold.
How I've learned to shine
not in spite of my pain,
but because of it.

We'll talk
like souls
remembering each other

and that conversation
will carry us
Home.

On the Edge of Becoming

I feel the subtle,
dragging ache
of something new
taking root.

The quiet discomfort
that signals growth
not loud,
but undeniable.

A gentle tug
from somewhere deep within,
pulling me forward,
inviting me inward.

This is the ache of becoming.
The sacred stretch
between who I've been
and who I'm becoming.

A new chapter
awaits.
A new perspective
begins to unfold.
A new identity
rises
from the ashes of the old.

And though I can't quite name it yet,
I feel it
like light pressing
through the seams
of what once was.

There is a moment,
offered to me now,
to pause.
To honor the path
that brought me here.

To thank every version
of who I've been
every season,
every shedding,
every scar
because they prepared me
for this quiet becoming.

Something new
is taking form
in the unseen spaces.

A silent creation,
taking root
in fertile ground
warm,
dark,
sacred.

I can't put my finger on it.
The specifics remain blurred.
But the sensation is
so real,
so present,
so alive
beneath the surface.

This is emergence.

Undeniable.
Unstoppable.
Unfolding.

There's nothing I need to do,
no effort I need to exert.

No pushing.
No forcing.
No proving.

Just breath.
Just presence.
Just trust.

So I listen.
I soften.
I open.

And I walk barefoot
into the unknown
heart open,
eyes ready to see.

I invite it in.
This new life.
This becoming.

And I allow it.

I allow it all.

Loose Grip

I've learned
to hold my dreams
and goals
with a loose grip

not because I've stopped believing,
but because I've started trusting.

No matter what my mind
thinks it wants,
there is another kind
of emergence
happening within me
quiet, sacred, sure.

It moves me
not toward where I planned to go,
but toward where I'm meant to be.
Where I'm needed.
Where I'll see
what I couldn't see before.

Each detour waters
a hidden seed
of possibility
planted deep in my becoming.

And still
I dream.

I move with the vision
of a future
I can't yet name,
one I won't fully understand
until I arrive.

And when I do,
I know
just as gently,
just as surely,
I'll be moved
Again.

Questions

"What does it mean
to you
to live the questions
of your being?"

What questions
am I living now
often without realizing?

What questions
might be inviting me
into deeper places
of love,
life,
and longing?

What subtle invitations
into aliveness
do I stumble upon
each day
in a glance,
a breath,
a bird's song?

What stirs love
within me?
Around me?
For me?

What moves me
not just forward,
but inward?

What brings me
that sudden, swelling current
of joy and knowing,
the feeling of being
fully
alive?

What is calling
to me
right now
in this very breath?

What is awakening
beneath the noise?

What sensations
have I ignored
in the name of productivity,
in the pursuit
of doing?

How can I return
to being
more fully,
more honestly,
more me?

How do I remember
who I truly am
when everything
I thought I was,
dissolves
into warm,
murky,
sacred darkness?

And what am I becoming
as I rise
into the white light
of life,
of truth,
of soul?

When do I feel
most connected?

When do I hear
the gentle whispers
of something ancient
and eternal
within me?

What is seeking
to be born
through me?

What is already
moving inside me
unfolding quietly,
patiently,
toward the light?

What moments
draw that energy
to the surface
until it bubbles over
into form
creativity made visible
from the invisible
wellspring within?

What music
is playing
in the raw,
unwritten room
of my soul?

What questions
are mine
to live?

What questions
are mine
to love?

What Matters?

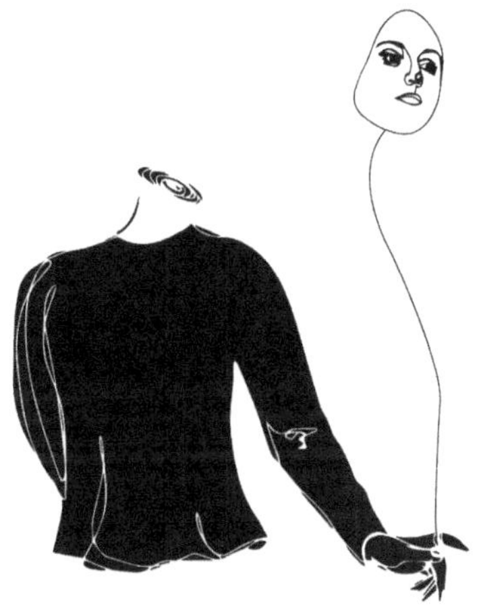

The salty teardrops
on my face
remind me of something.

Something ancient.
Something sacred.

But I don't know
what I'm trying
to remember.

What matters?

Maybe it's that ache
that silent knowing
deep in my chest
that there is something here.
Something real.
Something hidden
just beyond
plain sight.

What matters?
Not the notifications
that claw at my nervous system,
stealing sleep
and stillness.

Not the titles,
not the timelines,
not the performance
of having it all together.

What matters?
Maybe it's the pit in my stomach
that whispers
This isn't it.

Maybe it's the way
my body speaks
what my mouth still won't say.

What matters?

I'm here with myself
and I see.

I see the fragments
of who I thought I was.
The roles I played.
The versions I performed.

And I wonder:
What is actually me?
What am I still trying to be?

I play dress-up in my own skin.
I wear masks
so carefully constructed
to keep the world comfortable.

But she's in there
the real me.
Screaming.

I'm screaming inside.

A loud and piercing sound
I've learned how to muffle.
How to disguise
with smiles and spreadsheets,
lipstick and leadership.

Shhhhhhhh.

What matters?

That voice inside
that won't be silenced anymore.
The ache that tells me
there is something truer
beneath the surface
of all this striving.

This mask is getting heavy.
And I'm tired.

So tired.

I feel the storm building
dark clouds swirling
beneath my ribs.
The world feels
upside
down.

I cry.
Again.

I still don't know
what I'm trying to remember.
Only that something
has been lost.
And that it's mine.

There's a barrier
between me and me
but it's thinning.
And I can feel
the truth breaking through.

What matters?

The way he looks at me
when I'm truly present.
The quiet desire
for something I haven't yet named.
The stillness I avoid
and secretly crave.

What matters
is this ache
to belong
to myself.

The beauty of being.
The pain of remembering.
The shimmer of truth
rising
from the wreckage
of everything I was never meant to be.

What matters
is that I'm still here
searching, seeing,
and slowly,
becoming.

A Poem for Remembering

Past.

Present.

Future.

Future.

Present.

Past.

The Earth knows
these are not separate.
Not really.
She holds them all
in the same breath.

She is well-versed
in the language of cycles,
of birth and decay,
of death becoming life
again.

She feels the endings
in every beginning.
She feels the beginnings
in every ending.
They dance together
intertwining
eternally.

Spirit rises
with the birds,
with the wind,
with the stars.

While Soul
roots itself
deep in the dark,
fertile belly of the Earth.

We are beings
of both realms
sky-bound and soil-born.
Light and matter.
Heaven and humanness.

At home in the unseen.
At home in the soil.

Learning to honor both
this is the sacred work
of an eternal existence.

To remember
the Earth's memory.
To participate
in her dreaming.
To walk gently
on the skin of a planet
that has always held us

even when we forgot
how to listen.

These are
our divine tasks.

To remember
that beginnings and endings
are not opposites
but mirrors.

That the middle
always carries us
back
to the edge
of something new.

To remember
that the Earth
is a teacher,
and we are her students
if we choose to hear.

We must
remember the conversations

between trees and beings.

We must
remember the whispers
Remained in silence,
those soft pulses
beneath the noise
that speak
without words.

We must
remember the way
we once knew
how to belong
to this place.

Remembering
is our divine task.

Unintentionally Reinforcing a Broken System

I tell myself
the work I'm doing matters.

But does it really?

Sure
we help people.
We offer comfort.
We teach tools.

We soothe symptoms.

We help people cope
with a world that is
still burning.

But too often,
we offer solutions
before we honor the pain.

We unintentionally
invalidate their suffering
by trying to fix it
too quickly.

We subtly reinforce
the belief
that they are the problem.

That they must change
to fit into
a system that was
never made
to hold them whole.

We don't mean to
but we do.

We tell them
we know how to help.
We say it with
our degrees,
our programs,
our polished words.

But sometimes,
I don't even know
how to help myself.

Their pain
is my pain.
Their exhaustion
echoes in my bones.
Their despair
lives under my skin, too.

And here's the truth:
All of it is okay.

The Pain.
The Rage.
The Grief.

But no one talks about that.

No one says:
You have a right to be angry.

No one says:
It's okay to fall apart.
It's okay to cry in front of me.
I cry, too.

When they say they feel despair,
I believe them.
Because I feel it, too.

It lives
in the air we breathe.
In the silence of meetings.
In the margins of policies.
In all these unexamined
structures we work within.

We say we want
a better world.

But few are willing
to burn the broken one down.

Few are ready
to name the systems
we reinforce
in the name of healing.

Few are ready
to ask:
What if their pain
is wisdom?
What if our job
is not to fix it,
but to feel it
together?

The Other Reasons

The reasons you wake up every morning
not your alarm clock.
Not the deadlines or to-do lists.

The other reasons.

The quiet pull
on your heartstrings
guiding you
toward places
still unknown.

The flicker in your gut
when something deep inside
whispers:
This matters.

The thoughts
you carry like stars
on long drives and sleepless nights
about why we're here,
and what it all means.

The teardrops
you didn't expect
sacred and sudden,
reminding you
of the fragile magic
woven into every single moment.

These are the other reasons
we rise each day.

Not the job.
Not the title.
Not the masks we wear
to belong.

But the breath that fills you
when you stop running.
The wave of aliveness

that swells
when you let yourself
feel.

The breaking open
that reveals
the light beneath the dark.

The perspective shift
when your own story
starts to shimmer
in a new way.

The way you remember
you are more
than one thing.

You are
fascinating.
Confusing.
Magical.
A living paradox.

These are the reasons
we forget sometimes

when we get lost in time,
in noise,
in motion.

But they're always there,
waiting quietly
beneath the surface.

The other reasons.
The real ones.
The ones that bring us
back
to life.

Outsider Inside

Living in a world
that doesn't quite feel like mine.

Trying to belong
to this place,
this time
like slipping into a costume
that almost fits,
but itches at the seams.

They keep telling me,
You're in the right place.
You belong here.

You're doing great.

But am I?

I'm an outsider, inside.

I look the part.
I speak the language.
I show up
smiling,
strong,
professional.

But inside
it doesn't feel like my truth.

This world isn't my world.
At least,
not the whole of it.

Still, I try to fake it.
To force my shape
into spaces
never made
for all of me.

I try to be part of this world.
To blend in.
To be enough.
To make it make sense.

But somewhere inside,
a quieter voice says:
This isn't it.
You're from somewhere else.
You remember something more.

So I ration my soul
showing only the safe pieces.
Tiny glimmers of who I am
get to come out and play,
while the rest
waits patiently
at home
on a shelf.

My friend reminds me,
Your worth isn't tied to your work.

But still,
I push.

Why does it take so much effort
just to be here?

Why does my heart
feel homesick
in a place I'm told
I'm meant to belong?

I don't have all the answers.
But I know this:

I come from somewhere deeper.
Somewhere softer.
Somewhere where I don't have to try so hard.

And maybe
just maybe
part of my work
isn't to fit in,
but to remember
what I came here
to bring.

I'm an outsider, inside.
But maybe that's not a flaw.
Maybe that's the truth.
Maybe that's the gift.

From First Embracing Chaos

Maybe

what I'm seeking
isn't peace,
or calm,
or perfect order.

Not yet, anyway.

Because to say
I'm at peace
with the way things are
would be a lie.

I don't want to live
in a protective bubble,
sealed off,
sweetly detached,
blind to a world
still burning.

Maybe what I'm truly longing for
is the courage
to embrace the chaos

within,
without.

The chaos.
The paradox.
The disruption.
The ache.
The trembling.

Both inside me
and around me.

I want to keep
my eyes open

and see.

All of it.

All that is broken,
All that is beautiful,
All that is unbearable,
and still breathing.

Eyes open
it's not pretty.

It's chaos.
It's contradiction.
It doesn't make sense.

How can love
exist beside greed?
Hope beside despair?
Joy beside injustice?

And yet
they do.
They always have.

I want to feel
the hollowness
carved by all that came before
the absence,
the sorrow,
the stories
still echoing.

I don't want to cover it
in glitter and platitudes.
I don't want to silence it
with spiritual clichés.

I want to stand
in the center of the storm
not untouched,
but alive.

I want to straddle
this strange, sacred reality
we've inherited
where beauty blooms
in the soil of suffering,
and still,

we rise.

There is beauty.
Yes.
I feel it.
I trust it.
I see it.

And there is ugliness too.
And I will not look away.

Not from the grief.
Not from the injustice.
Not from the uncomfortable truths
that ask more of me.

Because I know:
Solutions
are never born
from blindness.

A new way of being
a new world
can only rise

from first
embracing
chaos.

All Loose Ends

She said,
"I don't want to tie anything up.
I want all loose ends."

No bows.
No neat conclusions.
No freshly packaged
"new beginnings."

Just
all loose ends.

And how freeing
to know
we don't have to resolve everything,
don't have to wrap it all up
with a ribbon
just to make it digestible.

We can leave threads hanging
dangling,
spiraling,
becoming.

We can let the unfinished
breathe.

Because the loose ends
are where creativity slips in,
where possibility waits patiently,
where nothing is decided
and everything
is still alive.

Nothing is tidy.
And maybe,
nothing needs to be.

It's all
a beautiful mess
and maybe that's the most
honest thing
we could ever offer.

I told her,
"I love that.
To all loose ends
the poems,
the people,
the parts of ourselves
still becoming."

To all loose ends.
To all that's still unfolding.
To the art
of not knowing.

On Her Way to Me

When I look back
and read
what I was writing
only six years ago,
I meet a long-forgotten sorrow
a broken-hearted girl
who didn't yet know
how much she had to grieve
Before reaching gratitude.

I forgot
how much I had to feel,
to lose,
to break open
before I could find
the light in me.

I look back,
and the memory echoes
with the ache of becoming—
with lessons
just beginning
to unravel.

I was descending
into the underbelly
of my own shadow,
face-to-face
with the beast inside me
and somehow,
I made it through.

The same,
and profoundly different.

I wouldn't recognize that girl now
except for the love
she always carried
in her heart.

She's grown
into something
more spacious,
more self-compassionate,
more forgiving.

But it didn't happen
all at once.

It happened breath by breath,
scar by scar,
one bleeding heart
at a time.

She came home
into me.

She became whole.
She became free.

And now,
looking back
I think she knew.

Even in her suffering,
even when it felt endless
somewhere deep inside,
she knew
she was on her way
to me.

To the Little Girl

To the little girl
who didn't feel safe,
who learned to hide
within herself

I want you to know,
even though
there are still many years
of aching ahead,

your story
turns out
beautifully.

You learn to love
the broken parts of you
the ones you used to fear,
used to silence,
used to tuck away.

And not only do they heal
they shine.
They shimmer with wisdom,
casting light into spaces
where others still wander.

You learn to listen
to the voice that matters
the one inside your soul.
And even when you feel weak,
you stand strong.
You keep going.

You never stop
seeing beauty
in everything.

Heartbreak will find you
a few more times

than you'll like
but each one
will carve out space
for deeper love.
The kind that stays.
The kind that was always meant
to last.

You let go
of trying to be anything
other than who you are.

And one day,
you'll just be.

Free.
Seen.
Soft and bold
all at once.

You'll learn to set down
your worried mind
and step fully
into wonder's eye.

You'll draw.
You'll paint.
You'll write.
You'll dance barefoot
in the moonlight
and whisper secrets
to the stars.

You'll stand tall
not in defiance,
but in truth.

Rooted in yourself,
you'll see others
for who they are,
even when they can't
yet see themselves.

And no
your story isn't over,
my dear.

But it gets better,
It gets softer,
It gets brighter
every day.

Anyway,
I just wanted to write to you
to say,

you're going to be okay.

Can You See Me Now?

Don't tell me,
"You're beautiful."
Don't tell me,
"I love your hair."
Don't comment on my weight,
my size,
my body's current shape.

I know
you mean it with love.
I know you're reaching
for a connection.
I know you're trying

to lift me up,
and this feels better
than the ways
we were taught
to tear each other down.

But the kind of connection
I long for
lives deeper
than the surface of my skin,
this skin
I was taught
my worth was wrapped in.

Compliment my words.
Admire my strength.
Notice my essence.
Witness my light.

See me.
Not the vessel
but the soul inside.

Yes, this body is sacred.
It is powerful.

It is resilient.
It holds my story.
But it is not
all
of me.

This obsession
with how we look,
this drowning fixation
on bodies
it leaves me aching
for more.

It isolates.
It objectifies.
It keeps us from
meeting soul to soul.

I'm not asking
to be ignored
I'm asking
to be seen.

Seen for my mind,
my energy,
my contradictions,
my curiosity.

I am complex.
Messy.
Paradoxical.
Deep.

So I ask you
to see what I'm offering.

See the fire.
See the ache.
See the brilliance
and the becoming.

See the way I love.
The way I listen.
The way I walk through the world
with softness and steel.

Not just this body.
Not just this shell.

See me.

You Can't Guarantee

You can't guarantee
that I'll wake up tomorrow.
That I'll rise with the sun,
feel its golden warmth
on my skin,
and remember
what a miracle it is
just to breathe.

You can't guarantee
that I'll hear the call
the one that sings
my name
so softly,

so fiercely,
it pulls me
into the deepness of things.

You can't guarantee
that I'll know who I am
when the question becomes
too sacred
to ignore.

You can't guarantee
that I'll stay awake
long enough
to witness
my own becoming.

You can't guarantee
that I'll taste love
on my lips
or remember
the color of passion
when the world
sweeps me away
in routine
and small talk

and endless
to-do lists.

You can't guarantee
that I won't forget
the very things
I came here for
that I won't trade
the mystery
for the performance,
the soul
for the script.

You can't guarantee
that I'll know you
when I see you again.
I might forget.

Maybe I already have.

But I guarantee this

Even in forgetting,

even when I fall asleep
to my own truth,

I already am.

The light,
the question,
the pulse,
the presence
still lives in me.

Even when I lose the way,
I am the way.
Even when I forget,
something inside me
remembers.

I already am.

To My Mother

Growing up,
I only knew you
in relation to me
as the role you played,
the protector,
the provider,
the one called
"Mom."

And because of that,
I often failed to see
the radiant complexity of you
the woman beyond the name.

The beauty.
The challenge.
The desire.
The destiny
that pulsed within you
long before I arrived.

But I see it now.

I see the way you rose
to every challenge life offered
not always perfectly,
but always
with heart.

With love.
With the intention
to create something
worth remembering.

I see the way
you held your own hurts
while you held us,
trying to shield us

from the very world
that wounded you.

I see the fierce protection,
the advocacy,
the fight in your bones
when it came to doing
what you felt was best.

I see the love
you poured out,
and the love
you sometimes forgot
to pour back into yourself.

I see how you never gave up
on love,
on life,
on the flicker of something more.

Even with the burden,
the weight,
the stories you didn't choose
but carried anyway.

You kept hoping.
You kept believing.
You kept searching
for beauty
in a world that so often
showed you pain.

But most of all
I see now
that there was always
a river of mystery
running through you,
quiet and sacred,
that none of us
were ever meant
to fully know.

I see how you carried
your heartbreak
in silence,
how you wore strength
like a second skin.

And still
you danced.

You sang.
You lit candles in the dark
and called it joy.

You connected to your fire
even when life
tried to extinguish it.

I like to think
I get that from you

that undying hope,
that dreaming mind,
that dancing spirit,
that unbreakable spark.

And if I carry even one ember
from your fire
into the world,

I will be proud
to be your daughter.

To My Sister

When I look at you,
I see only magic
twinkling in your eyes,
shimmering in your skin,
sparkling through your laughter
like sunlight on water.

Pure magic,
radiating from
deep within.

You shine so brightly,
you sometimes blind yourself
forgetting the power
that pulses through you
with every breath.

But I see it.
I see you.

I see how you shine,
how you burn,
how you move through this world
with fierce grace
sharp,
brilliant,
unapologetically alive.

You slice through the noise
with truth in your gaze
and joy in your voice.
You cast spells
with your laughter
lifting the veil,
lightening the air.

You breathe in fairy dust
and exhale wonder.
You hold the secret
of this life
like a compass
in your heart.

You know what I know
that we are more
than skin and story,
more than roles or rules
or what the world sees.

You hold the knowing
that life is too short
to miss a single
glimmer.

And you don't.
You hold it.

The sacredness of now.
The sacredness of us.
This bond
timeless, cosmic,

written in the stars
and etched into the marrow
of our becoming.

Whether you are near
or far,
I feel you.
I carry you.
Your magic mind
has always been with me,
through space,
through time,
through every version of ourselves.

So if ever you forget
if the world dulls your shine
or you lose sight
of what lives in you

I will be here
to remind you:

The magic you seek
isn't out there.

It's you.
It has always been
You.

To My Best Friend

I don't think
I would have survived
my teenage years
not whole,
not breathing,
not me
without you
by my side.

You were the anchor
in the storm,
the one who always knew
how to make me feel

seen
Normal.
Known
into being.

I've never felt judged by you
and let's be honest,
those early years
gave you plenty of stories
that could have inspired judgment.

But you gave me grace.
You gave me space.
You knew me
even while I was stumbling
through the mess
of becoming.

And still
you stood by me.

I've always admired
your grit,
your grace,
your brilliance,
your quiet strength.

No matter what came,
you stood tall,
regal,
certain,
like you already knew
who you were
and where you were going.

And I watched you
prove yourself right.

You are dazzling,
determined
and wise beyond your years.

You are a fiercely loyal,
honest,
unshakable friend.

The kind that people hope for
and the one I was lucky enough
to have.

You've seen me
in every season
at my lowest,
my most lost,
and my most radiant.

And through it all,
you stood steady.
Present.
Kind.

You were the one constant
I could count on
when everything else
was unraveling.

You helped shape
who I was,
who I am,

and who I'm still becoming
not through pressure,
but through presence.

Because of who you are,
I felt safe enough
to grow.

Even in the darkest chapters,
the time we shared
was light.

It was Popcorn and Mountain Dew,
Cookies and movie nights.
It was the sound of belonging
when everything else
felt too loud.

And now,
we are women
no longer girls
and I couldn't be more proud
of the life
you've created
from scratch.

You are an inspiration.
A sister.
A forever friend.
A kindred soul
who has always
seen me clearly.

The world is better
because you exist.

And I
I am better
because I've known you.

Because you've known me.

To My Soul Mate

You know who you are
the one who woke the light
in my life.
The one who looked at me
and called me
Moon Eyes.

Thank you
for being such
a delightful surprise.

When I found you,
I learned what it truly meant
to be alive.

You lit a fire in me
not the kind
that scorches and destroys,
but the kind that warms
cold hands
and aching hearts.

The kind of fire
that stays.
That glows.
That endures.

Steady.
Hot.
True.

I know this journey
called life
dealt us both
a complicated hand.

But together,
we built a dreamscape
from the rubble
a world of color,
laughter,
and deep rest.

We create.
We play.
We love.
We pause.

We make each moment
sacred
just by choosing it.
Just by being here.

Thank you
for saying "I love you"
often,
and like you mean it
every time.

Thank you
for holding me

close
especially on the days
I couldn't hold myself.

Thank you
for seeing me
not just for who I was,
but for who I was becoming.

For believing in me
when I forgot how.
For whispering hope
into the parts of me
that still trembled.

You opened
my heart,
my mind,
my soul
to what love could be.
To what it means
to be truly known.

Thank you
for staying

while I healed.
For not flinching
at my fears.

Thank you
for living your life
as your own
boldly, freely,
beautifully
and showing me
how to do the same.

You reminded me
to look beyond
the surface of things,
to notice
beauty in the smallest moments,
to savor
the art of ordinary joy.

To play.
To rest.
To be.

Our souls
they were built
for each other.

And every single day,
I am grateful
for the life
we've made.

The sacred,
silly,
steady,
soulful life
we get to share.

To My Brothers

I don't think I tell you
enough
how much I love you,
how often I think of you,
how grateful I am
to call you mine.

Watching you grow
in your own ways,
becoming the men
you were always meant to be,
has been a quiet honor
a gift I carry
even from afar.

Each one of you
brings your own light
your own laughter,
your own kind of magic
to this world.

And though you move
in different rhythms,
different stories,
different lives,

to me,
you will always
share something sacred:
the role of brother.

And what a blessing it is
to have not just one,
but three
men in my life
who love me
like only brothers can.

We don't always have
the time to connect,

or the language
to fully understand
each other's day-to-day.

But still
there's a knowing.

A thread that ties us
through memory,
through childhood,
through the deep-rooted bond
of having grown up
side by side.

And no matter
how long it's been
or how far we've wandered,
when I see you again
it's like no time
has passed at all.

We fall right back
into the rhythm
of our shared story:
familiar laughs

and a love
that never needed
to be explained.

In you,
I have not just brothers
but friends.

Thank you
for being a part
of the foundation
that shaped me.

Thank you
for your presence,
your resilience,
and your place
in my heart
Always.

To the Future Leader

I hope you hold
the hearts and minds
of those you serve
in your work,
and in your life
with tenderness,
with presence,
with loving care.

I hope you lead
not just with answers,
but with awareness.

Because what people need
isn't perfection.

They don't need you
to have it all figured out,
to solve every problem,
or carry every burden.

They need you
to see them.
To be with them.
To walk beside them
in the uncertainty.

They need your honesty.
Your integrity.
Your vulnerability.
Your truth.

They need to know
that your values
aren't just words
they are lived,
embodied,
and brave.

I hope you've spent time
tending to your inner life

because whatever lives within you
will ripple
into every room you enter.

I hope you know
your own shadows.
Your patterns.
Your triggers.
Your trauma.

I hope you've made peace
with the parts of you
that once led from fear.

I hope you've practiced
the art of saying "I'm sorry,"
of making repair,
of choosing humility
over ego.

Because the leaders we need
today and tomorrow
aren't those who fix everything
they're the ones
who feel everything,

who stand with people
in both challenge and celebration.

The ones who don't rise above,
but rise with.

Who don't command power,
but cultivate trust.

Who don't just direct
but invest.
Deeply.
Honestly.

In people's wholeness.
In their growth.
In their truth.

So if you're reading this,
and you haven't yet
done your inner work

Let this be your sign.

Now is the time.

Because the future doesn't need
another perfect leader.

It needs a present one.

GED

G. E. D.
Three letters
that once filled me
first with pride
then, quietly,
with shame.

When I think about
the things I don't advertise,
the stories that hide
behind the polish
of my higher degrees
this one comes to mind.

GED.

I used to bury it
beneath academic accolades,
behind credentials,
certificates,
letters after my name.

But I'm not doing that anymore.
Not here.
Not today.

Because the truth is
I dropped out of high school.
Not because I didn't care,
but because I needed to work.

I got a job at Finish Line,
selling sneakers and socks,
upselling shoe cleaner kits
like my life depended on it
because, in some ways,
it did.

At that time,
it made sense.
Leaving school
felt like freedom.
Like survival.

And when I realized
I wanted more,
more choice,
more possibility,
more voice,
I went back.

I studied alone.
Quietly.
Determined.
And I passed.

That piece of paper—
the GED
was my gateway.

It opened the doors
to every degree
that followed.

It reconnected me
to learning,
to purpose,
to possibility.

But I didn't talk about it.
Because I learned
that "equivalency"
doesn't always feel
equal in the eyes
of the world.

I heard the subtle judgment.
Saw the raised brows.
Felt the sting
of surprised silence.

So I stopped sharing.

But not anymore.

GED.

This poem
is my release.

A quiet truth,
finally spoken.
A reminder
to me,
to anyone listening

that our beginnings
don't define our becoming.

My path wasn't straight.
It wasn't easy.
But it was mine.
And it was powerful.

And none of what I've built
none of who I've become
would have been possible
without those three letters
that changed everything.

GED.

Proof
that grit
and grace
and growth
can take you
Anywhere.

Love Story

My Heart has borne
a quiet Bruise
The kind
that does not show
It breaks
and bleeds
yet learns again
to let the Longing grow.

A Battered thing
but Blooming still
It sought
in Lightening's Flame
The kind of Love

that strikes the Soul
and never leaves
the same.

My Early Years
were Lessons steep
To Love
I paid a Fee
A piece of Mind
a bit of Self
and fragments
of my Me.

I offered it
so Willingly
as if
to be made Whole
meant someone else
would need to hold
the Tender of my Soul.

But Tears
how they Visited
their Salt
upon my Skin

and every Time
I asked again
Is Love
a kind of Sin?

I thought perhaps
it must be me
Some Flaw
not yet Repaired
Some unworthy
Depth of Lack
Some wound
not meant to care.

But now I know
what I did not
in all those aching Years
That Pain invites
Reflection's truth
not just the Ghosts
of Fears.

For what we meet
in Others' Arms
is Echo

of our Pain
And only when
I loved Myself
could I be Loved
again.

I learned to speak
sweet Psalms
to me
to draw
a Bolder Line
To bless the Mirror
with my Gaze
and claim this Heart
as Mine.

And though
I found
a wondrous Love
A Soul
that met my Own
There is
a Greater
Tale
to tell

beneath
the skin and Bone.

It took
some Time
to See it clear
but now
I hold it fine

My greatest Love
was not out There
but always
always
Mine.

Identity

How many of me
are wrapped beneath my skin?

How many faces
wait to be named?

How many voices
speak when I listen?

How many truths
live quietly
beneath the ones I've shared?

How many of me
have already risen
and how many still sleep
beneath the surface
of becoming?

I have worn masks
and shed them.
I have softened
and sharpened
according to the season.

One me,
many tasks.
One soul,
a hundred mirrors.

I have learned
to love the ones I've met
the tender girl,
the fierce woman,
the shapeshifter
called to heal.

And I await
the selves I've yet to know
the ones who will arrive
not with answers,
but with invitations.

Each version
a teacher.
Each thread
part of the tapestry.

Who I was,
who I am,
who I will be

not separate,
but stitched together
in this skin,
this story,
this sacred unfolding.

Not finished
but forming.

Not fixed
but free.

I am not just one.
But Many.

Chilled to the Bone

Sometimes I get
so cold
I feel it in my bones.
A silent ache,
a hollow weight
that settles in alone.

Not just a chill
upon the skin
but something deeper,
buried in.

A gentle sorrow,
a quiet sting,
like holding something
frozen
too long in spring.

Or walking home
through icy rain,
each droplet echoing
some unnamed pain.

What brings warmth
when the soul feels numb?

Not blankets,
not candles,
not cups of hot rum.

Tea won't do
nor fleece-lined sleeves.
There's a colder ache
that never leaves
without a different kind of flame
a sacred heat

that has no name.

I need a fire
wild and true
to blaze within
and burn right through.

Not to destroy
but to ignite
the tender spark
of inner light.

So I will search
through ash and air,
through quiet breath
and whispered prayer
until I find
some ember small
that knows my name
and warms it all.

I'll feed it life.
I'll guard its glow.
And let it teach
my blood to flow.

I'll wrap that heat
around my core
and breathe again,
cold no more.

Soul Quest

An adventure out
to meet myself
and something more
I can't explain.

I've eaten clean,
detoxed my soul,
and prepped
for an interesting day.

My pack is filled
with water, cards,
crystals humming
soft and true.

I lace my shoes,
set out alone,
and know the Earth
is guiding too.

I walk and walk
'till time dissolves,
'till names and hours
disappear.

The birds begin
to speak in song
and suddenly
I belong here.

I find a tree
a witness still,
a sacred place to rest.

I speak my truth,
I share my past,
I put the tree
to test.

It listens well.
The silence holds.

My tears begin to pour.
A living altar,
deep and wise,
receiving all
I bore.

I lay down near
the water's edge,
its pull, both wild and sweet.
The breeze becomes
a lullaby,
the sand
a bed
beneath my feet.

I look above,
the sky so wide
and ask this ancient plea:
"Why am I here?
What is this life?
What is my soul to be?"

The air responds
not with a word,
but with a soft caress
a whisper caught
within the wind,
a hush of tenderness.

I wade into
the icy waves,
the cold, a sacred kiss.
I wash away
what came before,
and rise renewed
from this.

I wander dunes
and wooded paths,
my senses— sharp and bare.
The trees begin
to breathe and hum
there's meaning
in the air.

Then suddenly
a presence near,
the forest hushes low.
A doe appears
beside a stream,
pausing soft
and slow.

She drinks, then lifts
her gaze to mine
and in her eyes,
I see
a sister soul,
a mirror clear,
reflecting
back to me.

We are the same
wild and wise,
soft strength,
and untamed grace.
We share the same
unwritten code
of earth and time
and space.

I turn to go
my journey full,
yet something still remains.
And then
a flash of color bright,
a quiet, final flame.

A butterfly
blue-black and bold,
so regal, calm, and free
descends with grace
upon my crown
and whispers:
You are already She.

And in that moment,
on that shore,
the truth unfurled in me

My purpose
wasn't far away.
It lived
eternally.

Blood and Tears

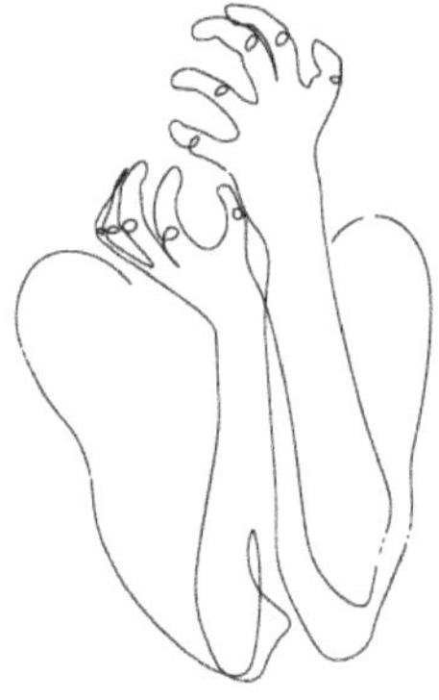

Sometimes I think back
to the night the veil thinned
when everything ordinary
broke open
and the world bent sideways
into something
unrecognizable.

It began like any other evening.
The moon was hanging,
a silver eye watching me
from behind the clouds.
My body moved through the motions
of another tired day.

But something ancient stirred.
Something that had been buried
under years of silence
and soft smiling lies.
And then
it happened.
The mirror caught my eye.
But the face wasn't mine.

It was the echo
of a girl I used to be
frightened, exhausted,
cracked from the inside.

My mind spun
like a storm.
My vision blurred.
I fell inward.

Blood and tears,
and bathroom towels
and something holy unraveling.

A death occurred
that no one else could see.
Not a death of body,
but of illusion.
Of performance.
Of pretending.

Someone died in the bathroom
that night.
And when I emerged
shaking,
half-born
I knew I would never be the same.

There was fire in me.
Not fury
but forge.

Through blood and tears
and sacred flame,
something new
was born.

A soul remembered.
A self reclaimed.

That night,
revelations pierced me
like lightning strikes
truths I had never dared to hold.
Heartbreak.
Heartache.

And the sobering realization:
the girl I had built to survive
was not the woman I was meant to be.

My father crossed my mind
and for a moment,
I understood the weight
he had carried.
I tasted the edge of despair.
I saw how easy
the slipping can be.

But I was not ready to die.
Not literally.
But yes
I needed to let something end.
I laid her down,
the former version of me.

I thanked her
for her fight,
for her fierce endurance,
for getting me this far.

And then I chose
to live.
To heal.
To rise.
To evolve.
To reclaim
the one precious life
still pulsing through my hands.

I crossed the threshold.
Naked.
Raw.
Reborn.

It all changed
that night.
I didn't break.
I burned bright.

Bloom

Our unfolding
doesn't follow a plan.
Our blooming
doesn't arrive
in one grand,
sudden,
miraculous moment.

No
to bloom is to become
in layers,
in pauses,
in spirals.

It happens slowly
one breath,
one ache,
one light-soaked morning
at a time.

Like the perennial
that returns stronger
with each passing year
so too do I.

Subtle.
Soft.
Cyclical.

Healing is not linear,
and wholeness is not rushed.
We learn,
we unlearn,
we fall,
we rise.
We make ourselves again
from tenderness.

We bloom like wine

deepening with time.
More textured,
more complex,
with layers quite divine.

And yet
we forget.

We grow impatient.
We demand clarity
before we're ready to see.
We plead for results
before the roots
have fully taken hold.

But the problem
is not in our pace.

It's in our lack of trust.

We push.
We force.
We cry.

Not realizing
the seed has already
been planted.

And that forceful hand
the one that tries to pull
the petals open too soon
is the very thing
that bruises the bloom.

It stifles
what was gently
trying to come alive.

The part of us
that rushes
is also the part
that aches
when things fall apart.

Because blooming
was never about
how fast you go,
or how much you know

but rather,
the grace
with which
you hold yourself
through each becoming.

Let it be gentle.
Let it be true.

You are not behind.
You are becoming.

And this,
this right here,
right now,
is part of your
bloom.

Moon Eyes

What if I gave a name
to my wild, mythic flame

the part of me
who runs with wolves,
screams in her wildness,
refuses to tame.
She dances freely
around the fire,
moves with instinct,
heart, desire.

The one
where passion lives and plays,
and childlike wonder
guides her days.

She loves like storms
that kiss the land
fierce and full,
a force unplanned.

She leans into what others fear,
laughs at rules,
then disappears
only to return with painted skies
and stars still burning in her eyes.

She sees your soul
and knows hers too.
She listens close
to earth, to you.
She speaks with creatures,
dreams with trees,
finds sacred messages
in the breeze.

Her wisdom wakes
when the world turns still,
beneath the moon
on the quiet hill.

She makes her wish
on falling light,
and trusts the magic
of the night.

She stares into
both sky and skin,
and names the galaxies within.

She moves the world
with softened power,
her blade a bold
and blooming flower.

She howls when broken,
screams her truth,
a voice of fire
since early youth.

She never chose
to walk the line
she bends the shape
of space and time.

This part of me
so long unnamed,
so wild, so brave,
so unashamed
waited quietly,
unseen, unknown,
until love made
her feel like home.

And then you came,
with soul-lit skies
and looked at her
with knowing eyes.

And in that gaze
the truth took flight
You called her
Moon Eyes
that night.

Enough Time

Sometimes
our bodies run amuck,
betray us with
a twist of luck.
A lump, a cyst,
a shadowed scan
the kind of thing
you think
can't touch your plan.

It's surely nothing.
A fluke. A lie.

A story meant
for other lives.

Still
you book the test,
you show up late,
heart in hand
and masked by fate.

Bright lights.
Cold tables.
A doctor's gaze
too still
and suddenly
your breath is caught
deep in your chest
against your will.

The poking,
The prodding
questions rise,
but answers
hide behind their eyes.

No clarity.

No final word.
Just a hush
a whisper
barely heard.

A dash of hope.
A cup of fear.
And the quiet question:
Am I still here?

The "what ifs" crowd
your once clear view.
And you wonder,
deep in shadow
Am I ready to say goodbye to this life?
To you?

You think of roles
you've yet to play:
mother, grandmother,
sage someday.
Professor. Teacher.
Elder wise
a woman who sees
with fire in her eyes.

You wonder
if your time was spent
in ways that mattered,
in love's intent.

Would the world take note
if you slipped away
or would it move on
without delay?

It's a sacred kind
of initiation
to meet your soul
in limitation.

To know it,
not through light alone
but in the moments
you feel most unknown.

So
you ask for presence.
You let fear in.
You make a quiet

peace with pain,
and let the grief
begin.

And then
a sigh.
A shift.
Relief.

Because when you trace
the lines of time
the love you gave,
the sacred climb
you find that even
if more awaits,
you've stood
inside
some golden gates.

And though your bones
still ache for more,
for songs unsung,
for open doors

You've known deep joy.
You've lived your truth.
You've felt your soul
in pain and youth.

And this becomes
your holy sign

That even if
the clock runs out,
you've already had

Enough time.

Swimming

There's nothing else that soothes
my body, mind, and soul
like water does
its gentle pull,
its rhythmic lull,
its holy, weightless hold.

Take me to the lake,
the ocean's wide expanse,
or even just a quiet pool
beneath the sun's soft glance.

I tread the water
like I'm pausing time
not here,

not yet,
a moment divine.

It holds me in
a sacred grace,
as droplets kiss
my upturned face.

Sometimes I wonder
in another life,
was I a creature
of the tides?
A dolphin, mermaid,
silver fish,
born of seafoam
and a wish?

It might sound silly
to say aloud,
but it feels like truth
beneath the sound.

I am more myself
when I am submerged,
than I have ever felt
on land.

I float
I'm light
I'm wholly free,
I'm wrapped in water's
memory.

I leave behind
the noise, the rush,
the tangled thoughts,
the world's loud hush.

My body becomes
wave and wind,
my breath a hymn,
my heart unpinned.

The water knows
it always has.
Its language flows
through fingers, past.

And my bones
remember this:
my birthright
of deep, embodied bliss.

Don't worry for me.
Don't check the time.
I've slipped inside
a sacred rhyme.

I'll be out here
for hours on end,
being schooled by the rain,
and held by a friend.

I wash it all
the doubts, the fears,
unspoken rules,
and find a blank slate
in cerulean pools.

No clocks,
no noise,
no deadlines to chase.

Only peace
and wild grace
to embrace.

And if you ask
why I'm all shiny and grinning,
I'll smirk and say
with stars still spinning:

"I'm swimming."

I Became Her

There were so many times
I needed a woman
strong,
fierce,
and kind.

A mentor.
A teacher.
A voice like balm.
A presence steady and calm.

Someone to stand beside me
as I stumbled through

the dark nights
of my soul
someone who knew the way
but wouldn't rush me through.

I searched the sky.
I searched the earth.
I prayed for signs
of sacred worth.

I wanted someone
to look up to,
a guide to light
the narrow way
someone who had once stood
where I now stood
and could assure me:
you will be okay.

I longed for wisdom
wrapped in softness,
for fierce compassion
and calm resolve.

I imagined her
with bright eyes
and calloused hands,
bearing stories of both
grief and gold.

But no matter how far
my gaze would roam,
I could not find
this soul outside.
I looked around
and found
just me.

And in that loneliness
a quiet gift.
A seed pressed deep
beneath the rift.

Solitude became my stone.
Silence became my guide.

And I made a list
every wish,
every aching prayer,

every trait I longed to see
reflected back to me.

I dreamed her up
this woman wise,
with fire in her belly
and stars in her eyes.

She was wild.
She was soft.
She was free.

And as the seasons shifted,
so did she.

I didn't notice
when it happened
at first
but somewhere between
the breath
and the breaking,

the learning
and the aching
the timeline blurred
and as if by magic

I became her.

I'm From Thick Thread

I am from the back porch,
where I used to dance
and sing
to no one
and to everything.

I am from the heartbreak
of my father
choosing to leave.

I am from suicide
and fading,
from the quiet resilience
of my mother
left to raise us
on her own.

I am born from strength
and saltwater tears,
from tragedy
and stone
like the little rocks
I used to collect,
souvenirs
from sun-drenched afternoons
spent outside alone.

I'm from bumble bees
and butterflies
I tried to keep alive
in plastic containers
we got from the dollar store
down the road.

I am from pants one size too small
and another hole found in my shoe.

I am from beauty
and insecurity,
from diet pills,
and fasts,
and apple cider vinegar
cleanses
that were never meant to last.

I'm from thick black eyeliner
from nail polish,
painted eyes,
and acetone.

I am from longing deep within
an aching desire to be known.

I am from quiet prayers
whispered in the dark,
my mother sitting beside me
at the end
of long, tired days.

I am from church donations,
from canned food
that kept us full
when we didn't know
how we'd make it
through the day.

I am from hand-me-down sweaters
and classmates' parents
who shared.
From the woman
whose house my mother cleaned
to pay the bills
to show she cared.

I am from grocery store lines
where the card didn't go through.
We'd put back this,
put back that
and I'd offer mine.

"No, it's okay. I don't need it."

I am from wonder
and awe,
from getting lost
inside the pages
of books that felt
like home.

I am from the belief
in magic,
from climbing trees
and stomping barefoot
in the rain puddles
that gathered
at the end of our driveway.

I am from front-yard igloos,
built with cold hands
and loud laughter,
from little joys
and loving hard.

I am from the kind of strength
that only comes

when you stand side by side
through life's hardest seasons
knowing you've kept each other alive.

I am from being known
in the purest way
from the unwavering love
in my mother's eyes.

I am from living room messes
and make-believe worlds,
from board games
and blanket forts
and stories told
at dark.

I am from here,
and there,
and everywhere—
and somehow
nowhere
all at once.

But mostly,
I am from the thick thread
that stitches together a life
strong, and worn,
and beautifully weathered.

A thread calloused
from worry,
softened by grace,
broken open,
broken down,
and built back up
from the ground.

What if I made mistakes

What if I chose to ignore
the voice that echoed wise?
What if I chose to turn away
when I needed to turn inside?

What if I chose the wrong
People to be around?
What if I only loved the ones
who would attempt to grind me down?

What if I let insecurities
run away and take the best of me?

What if I dropped out of high school?
What if I chose a lie
to tell myself each day
to enforce whatever

next wrong choice
I might decide?

What if I took out too many loans
and didn't spend them wise?

What if I let my impulses
Run away with my life?

Well, I'll tell you this
I've done all that
and somehow I've
made it to the other side

Because no matter what
choices my past self made
Eventually, I chose to feel alive.

There was no single
Mistake that was worth the cost of shame.
I've learned that all these choices
built the foundation on which
I was made.

I always did the best I could
with the tools I had at the time
and now I've learned to love that girl
who didn't have a guide.

I bring her with me,
wherever I go.
I have nothing to hide.

She is me
And I am her
And we are quite alright.

Broken

I want things whole
but I love things broken.

The broken things are
so much more interesting.
Cracked,
Damaged,
Frayed at the edges

what's broken
carries a heart,
a soul,
a story left untold.

Broken makes me curious.
It whispers
to my soul:

there's more to see.
It invites me in,
asks me to look closer.
To wonder.
To feel.
To stay.

Broken like a heart,
a vase,
a pair of glasses.
Broken like a lightswitch
that seems to control nothing
or maybe everything.

Broken like bones,
or glass,
or old costume jewelry
with a missing clasp.

Broken says:
I broke the rules.
I couldn't stay
the way I was made.

Broken says:
You won't find me here.
You'll find me there
where play lives,
where change begins.

Broken like the mug
I glued together
with clumsy care
its seams still showing,
but held,
still useful,
still beautiful
and rare.

Broken like the oven
after I made too much
for Thanksgiving dinner.

Broken mirrors.
Broken hearts.
Broken timelines.
Broken starts.

It's all so fascinating.
Because what breaks
never returns
the same.

And that change
that wild, irreversible change
feels like something holy to me.

Like the shift my soul made
when it entered this body.
Like the breaking open
of my mind
when I knew
I couldn't unknow
what I now see.

Brokenness
creates space.

I've felt it
the shattering.
The crumbling to the floor.
The ache that said:
I can't

stay
this broken
anymore.

And still
I know this truth:
what's broken
becomes
something new.

Even though the breaking hurts

I think
it was always
meant to.

I Won't Go Back There

I won't go back there this time
to the creaky floors
and dim-lit stairs,
to the damp breath
of walls that whisper
what I've spent years
unlearning.

I won't relive that darkness
where water trickled
from the light sockets,
where shadows moved
without bodies,
and ghosts
took up residence upstairs.

I won't go back there.
Not again.

Not to the hiding
beneath the bed,
clutching breath,
praying not to be heard.

I won't go back,
and you can't make me try.
Not for resolution.
Not for empathy.
Not even to prove
how far I've come.

It's not worth reliving
the pain that lives
in that place.

I'd rather look forward
eyes wide,
heart steady
than step once more
into that fractured space.

That place
where fear learned
its name.
Where innocence
slipped
through floorboards.
Where the timeline split
and something in me
cracked.

I won't go back
to the rats in the walls—
the soft clicking of claws
marking time
like a metronome
for dread.

I won't go back
to where I felt
most alone—
and wished to be
even more alone.

Where silence
meant danger,
and trust
was a trick
you learned too late.

I won't return.
And I don't need to.

Because healing
doesn't always ask
that we revisit
every room.

Sometimes,
we simply say no.
And mean it.

Sometimes,
we survive
by stepping forward
not by turning around.

And I'm stepping forward
now.

Not as the girl
who hid,
but as the woman
who walked out.

I won't go back there.

Not now.
Not ever.
Not even to look.

I carry what I need.
The rest
stays behind.

What I Save

What do you save?
What did your mother save?
Your grandfather?

I save memories.

I save art supplies
and ticket stubs.
Cards from friends,
family,
lovers.

I save books
and the thoughts
that woke up in me
when I read them
for the first time.

I save notebooks,
pages bursting with
ideas,
fears,
and flashes of brilliance
I forgot I ever had.

I save socks
with no match,
and clothes
that no longer fit
but once did.

I save rocks
from the beach
and sticks
that look like people.

I save plants
and I help them
thrive.

My mother saved
photographs,
albums,
and stories
she told again and again
with the same
glimmering excitement
every time.

She saved
the art we made,
the homework
that made her proud,
the moments
that made us
real
to her.

I don't know
what my grandmother saved.
I never got to know her,

though I always
wished I did.

Maybe
I am like her
in some quiet way
saving something
she once held dear,
without ever knowing
her hands
once held it too.

And maybe
I save
because I believe
nothing sacred
should be forgotten.

Because meaning
lives
in the things we keep.

Because something in me
wants to remember
what love looked like
when it was small
enough
to hold.

Part One: What I Always Wanted to Tell You

What I always wanted to tell you
was
I don't like
the person I see
in the mirror.

I don't like
the dimples in her thighs,
the softness around her waist,
the way her body folds
and lingers
in places I was taught
it shouldn't.

I always wanted to tell you
so you could really see me
not the version I present,
but the one who lives
beneath the smile.

The one who isn't
as confident
as she pretends to be.

I pinch myself.
I poke.
I suck in.
I shift.
I contort.
I try.

I try to be
"beautiful."
I try to be
"thin."
I try to be
enough.

I always wanted to tell you
so maybe
you could help me.
Maybe if you knew
you'd remind me
how to be kind.

I know
this isn't okay.
I know
these words
aren't true.

But still
I scold myself
daily.
Quietly.
Cruelly.

And I'm tired
of pretending
this isn't happening.

Part Two: What I'm Learning to Tell Her

But now
I am learning
to speak to her
softly.

To hold her
with the same reverence
I offer others.

To meet her in the mirror
not with war
but with wonder.

I've come to see
that her dimples
are part of her rhythm.
That the curve of her waist
is the place
where life leans in.

That her softness
isn't a flaw
it's a prayer
answered
in flesh and breath.

I don't suck in anymore.
I don't shape-shift
to please the gaze
of a world
that profits from my shame.

I catch the old voices,
but I no longer
bow to them.

I wear what feels like me.
I dance when no one's watching.

I eat when I'm hungry.
I rest when I'm tired.

I place my hand
over the skin
that once felt like
a battlefield
and now feels like
home.

I am not always
at peace
with her
but I am no longer
at war.

And that,
I've learned,
is enough.

I don't need
to be fixed.

I was never broken.

I just needed
to come back
to the truth
that this body,
this beautiful, wild,
tender body

is mine.
And she is worthy
of my love.

I See You

I get lost
in your dark brown eyes.

Not lost like confused
lost like found.
Like the world
makes more sense
when I'm looking at it
through the warmth of you.

When I look at you,
I see everything
I want to be
brave,
steady,
free.

I see you
with your head held high,
your heart wide open,
your independence intact.

I see the way you speak
with conviction,
the way your silence
holds space
for truth.

You don't try to fit,
you belong
exactly where you are.

And sometimes,
I wish I could see the world
from your eyes,

just to understand
how it feels
to be that full of fire
and grace
at the same time.

What I always wanted to tell you
is that you are capable
of more than you know—
that your gifts
spill out of you
without you even trying.

You paint with your voice.
You sing with your soul.
You breathe life
into blank pages,
into quiet moments,
into me.

I've watched you
from across the room
the way the light
falls differently
when you're there.

And I wanted to tell you,
always,
softly
I admire you.

Not from a distance,
but from the place
where love lives quietly
and waits to be named.

You are art
and anchor,
wild and wonder.

And I hope someday,
when you're ready,
you'll look into my eyes
and see
yourself
the way I do.

Stories I Used To Tell Myself

I'm not perfect.
I'm not "good."

I am a mess.
Tears on the floor.
Knots of emotion
twisting inside me
like thread too tight to breathe.

I am painful memories.
I am scars you can't see.
I am not polished.
Not clean.

Not tidy.
Not free.

And still
I try.
God, I try.

I chase that fantasy
of being enough
through perfection
as if being flawless
could make me
finally worthy
of rest.

I try to paint
a pretty picture of myself,
but the colors ring hollow
like a vase on a shelf
with nothing inside
but air.

And I know
you don't see me
for who I really am.

Because I'm still pretending.
Still performing.
Still wearing the smile
that fits just right
but feels
so wrong.

I hate this mask.
This weight of people-pleasing.
This aching hunger
to be liked
instead of real.

But I don't know
how to take it off.
Not yet.

I don't know
how to find my fate
without first
disappointing someone.

Without first
disrupting the image
they thought
was me.

What I'm Finally Telling Myself

You don't have to be perfect
to be worthy.

You don't have to hold it all together
to be loved.

You don't have to smile
when your heart is aching,
or shrink yourself
to make others comfortable.

You don't have to wear the mask
that never felt like home.

You can put it down now.
You can rest.
You can breathe.

You're allowed to take up space
exactly as you are
messy,
uncertain,
brilliant,
becoming.

Let the painting peel.
Let the colors run.
Let the vase shatter
if it needs to.

There is no beauty
in pretending.
There is only distance.

And you
you are meant for closeness.

For truth.
For a kind of soft
that does not bend
to be seen.

You are meant for the kind of life
that doesn't require
a performance.

And yes
it may take time
to learn how to be
without the mask.

To walk
without the weight
of who they needed you to be.

But you're already doing it.

With every honest breath.
With every quiet no.
With every brave moment
you choose to stay
with yourself

instead of abandoning her
for approval.

You're not lost.
You're arriving.
And this,
this is what it feels like
to come home,
to yourself.

I Want to Be Free

I'm in a play
Perfectly cast.
Performing the life
of someone
I never chose to be.

Sometimes,
a wave crashes through me.
I think it's truth
trying to wash the lies away.

But how do I escape
when I move in circles,
when every page unfolds
from invisible ink
I didn't know I was reading?

I am not free.
I am not free.
I am not free.
I am not free.

Every choice
already whispered
by unseen voices.
Every step
scripted in someone else's hand.

I don't want the role anymore.
I want the pen.
I want to write
my own wild script
but I don't know where
to begin.

What would it feel like
to walk the earth
bare and unburdened?
To be
without proving?
To exist
without performance?

Can I say goodbye
to my past,
to my future,
to even my name?

I don't want to go on
as "me."
Or as "you."

I just want to be.
Wild.
Sensual.
Unruly.

I want to dance
on the roadside,

freefall without a plan,
move like fire
and never look back.

I'm tired of pretending
I have answers.
No one does.
That's the truth.
There are no answers.

Everything just is
and isn't.
Dreams dissolve.
Reality slips.

In the dream realm,
I see her
a decapitated woman
floating in black water.

She is me.
The version I severed
to survive.

But all I want now

is to burn.
To feel the heat.
To glow under stars
like a sacred flame.

All I want
is to be free.

NO ONE KNOWS ME.

Not this me.
They know
the curated glimpse
the soft smile,
the safe light.

But what about the rest?
The wild, clumsy,
chaotic,
holy mess
I hide?

Where does she go
when I perform?
What would she say

if I let her speak?
Who would I become
if I stopped
trying to be—
Good?

One Day, the Words Come

One day,
the words come.

After years of silencing myself,
they arrive
like rain
after a long drought.

I don't know if today
is that day
but I trust
that it's coming.

One day,
I will awaken inside myself
and remember
I never had to hide
who I really was.

One day,
I'll say aloud
what I once only whispered
that I was raised
in secrecy,
in scarcity,
in a house that taught survival
was safer than truth.

I remember
my mother's voice
soft but urgent.
"When the teachers ask what you had for
dinner,

tell them your favorite meal.
Tell them pot roast."

We would nod.
We knew what was at stake.
They couldn't know
about the canned peas
from the church.
They couldn't know
that my brother sometimes
remained hungry.

They couldn't know
because if they knew,
someone might come.

So I said pot roast.
Always pot roast.
Even when my belly was hollow.
Even when I didn't mind
the peas
just the prayers
the strangers made us say
before handing over the food.

I preferred praying
with my mom at night.
She believed
it made things better.
I prayed,
but I wasn't sure
God was doing much at all.

Still, I placed my hand
on her back
when she cried,
and told her
it would be okay.

I went to school
with bruises,
scraped knees,
dirty fingernails.
Not from harm
but from barefoot tree climbing
and wild backyard adventures.

The guidance counselor
asked if I felt safe.
She smiled softly,

but I knew
what she wanted.

She wanted to take me away.
So I said very little.
Sometimes,
I asked to stay longer,
to play with her toys,
just to delay
the return to class.
She let me stay.

One day,
maybe these stories
won't feel
like shame.

Maybe,
I won't feel like a fraud
for now being
the kind of adult
who asks children
if they feel safe at home.

Maybe,
one day,
the words will come
to free me
from everything
I never said.

And maybe,
when they do
they'll sound
like healing.
Like release.
Like truth,
finally spoken,
without fear.

Wonder and Belonging

I know what wonder means.
I know how it feels
how it awakens something
ancient and electric
inside of me.

A deep memory,
ecstasy briefly remembered
in the smell of pine,
the sweep of wind,
the hush of stars.

Wonder lives in me.
It always has.

But tribe?
That word feels
less familiar.

What does it mean
to belong
to a people?
To be known,
not just loved
in the general sense,
but claimed
by others?

I've always done things
on my own.

I have friends.
Family I love deeply.
But I don't know
if I belong
to any one circle.

I think I've always
wanted to
but I keep parts
of myself
tucked away.

Guarded.
Hidden.
Not because I want to lie,
but because I'm afraid
of being misunderstood.

So even in a crowded room,
I wonder
do they know me?
Would they still love me
if they did?

This kind of loneliness
is quiet.
Intentional.

I don't always ask for help
when I need it.
I don't always say,

I'm overwhelmed.
Please come sit beside me.

I don't allow people
the chance
to be there.

And I don't fully know why.

Maybe it's a habit.
Maybe it's fear.
Maybe it's a myth
that strength
means solitude.

But a part of me
is ready
to stop disappearing.

To be known.
To be held.
To belong
not just in wonder,
but in the warmth
of being seen.

Recess

I remember being a child
at recess.

I always walked alone.

There was a yellow path
that circled the blacktop,
a loop I memorized
with the rhythm of my feet.

I would watch them
quick and quiet
carrying me
around and around
and nowhere in particular.

I can still feel
the cool air
on my cheeks,
the soft lining
of my coat pockets
where I kept my hands warm,
my thoughts warmer.

I can hear
the wind rustling leaves,
the chorus of kids
laughing,
shouting,
spinning in games
I never joined.

I stayed outside
the circle.
I don't know why,
not exactly.

Sometimes a child
would approach
"Do you want to play with us?"

And I'd smile,
always polite,
and say no.

I spent my recesses
elsewhere
in far-off lands
and future dreams,
wondering
who I might become
someday.

Even then,
I don't think
I trusted others
not to let me down.

I was afraid
they wouldn't like me
if I showed them
the whole truth
of who I was
the strange,
sensitive,
stormy child

beneath the surface.

And if I'm honest
a part of me
still feels that way.

The Circle I'm Creating Now

There was a time
I walked alone
circling blacktop paths
with my head down,
heart tucked
beneath zipped pockets.

But now,
I walk among a circle.

Not just near others
with them.

Beside them.
Held by them.

Now,
there are people
who know the real me
not the masked one,
not the polished parts,
but the whole
and holy
truth.

They see my softness
as strength.
They meet my sensitivity
with reverence.

And I don't have to ask
if I belong
I feel it
in the quiet nods,
the belly laughter,
the brave eye contact
when I say,
"I'm not okay."

and no one flinches.

This is the circle
I'm creating now.

One of honesty
and celebration,
of stories told in full voice
with no need to edit
the messy parts.

Now,
I don't walk the path alone.
I walk with women
who remind me
that being seen
can be sacred.

Now,
I don't turn down invitations
to play.

I make them.
I send them out
like prayers.

Like poetry.
Like reminders
that we were never meant
to do this life
alone.

The girl who once
daydreamed
about future belonging
she would marvel
at the life I live now.

She would weep
with relief.

And I would take her hand,
pull her gently
into the circle,
and say

Look around, sweet one.
We're finally home.

Let's Be Friends

I've been getting familiar
with the dark thoughts
the shadow parts I disowned.

I let them in.
I write them down.
I release them,
slowly.

It's not easy
to greet the shame,
to face the memories
I once tried to bury.

But I'm learning.

Each one arrives
with a whisper
"This is still here."

I used to turn away,
thinking neglect
would starve the pain.

But what I ignored
only cried louder,
only clung tighter,
only waited
to be seen.

So now I look.
I say
I see you, darkness.
You can come in.

Resistance still rises
a brick wall,
a firm "no."

But I can't leave
these stories
locked in the basement
of my body.

They are messengers.
Teachers.
Parts of me
longing for light.

So I open the door.
I dance with the dark
as I do with the dawn.

And something shifts
a freedom,
a quiet release.

I no longer abandon
what I used to judge.

The lump in my throat,
the fear in my gut
I welcome them.
I sit beside them.

I ask what they've come
to teach.

Greetings, anger.
Greetings, despair.
Greetings, compassion.
You're all invited here.

This life is a dinner party,
and I've decided
to stop hiding from myself.

Each moment,
I choose
to love
or abandon.

And I choose love.

I choose to hold
both sides
of my story,
because they both
belong to me.

Now That I Love Her

Now that I love her
everything has changed.

Not in loud, lightning-bolt ways,
but in small sacred ones.

Like the way I catch
my reflection
and smile
without editing.

The way I let my body rest
without guilt.

The way I speak to myself
like someone worth staying for.

Now that I love her,
I don't beg for proof
that I'm enough.

I know it
in the rhythm of my breath,
in the quiet trust
between my bones.

I touch the softness
of my belly
and feel gratitude
for the life she holds.

I see the fine lines
in the corners of my eyes
and trace them like a roadmap
to the joy I've earned.

I walk into rooms
without shrinking.
I show up
without apology.

I don't seek permission
to exist
anymore.

Now that I love her,
I don't measure her
by what she did
or didn't do.

I remember
how hard she tried
to be good
before she knew
she already was.

I hold that girl
the one who picked herself apart
and I whisper:
We're not doing that anymore.

We're dancing now.
We're resting.
We're creating.
We're laughing so hard
we forget
to be afraid.

She still shows up sometimes
that old ache
to be more.

But I know what to do now.
I wrap her in presence,
in praise,
in patience.

And she remembers
we made it.
We're home.
We're loved.

I look in the mirror
and say:

You're beautiful.
You are doing enough.
You are enough.

And this time,
I mean it.

We Want Something More

There is a hunger
growing louder each day
not for food,
but for something
real.

We want more
than the world we were given,
more than our histories,
our headlines,
our hollow routines.

We want more
than buzzing alarms
and long commutes,
than casual conversations
and shallow goodbyes.

We want to see a smile
and feel like we belong.
We want hands to hold,
souls to meet,
stories to tell,
And be heard.

We are sleep-deprived
and soul-starved,
wired and weary,
exhausted by proving
and performing.

We crave rest
that isn't earned,
love that isn't withheld,
connection that doesn't vanish
when the screen turns off.

We want something more.

We've tried to fill the ache
with sugar and scrolling,
caffeine and chaos,
lust and late nights.

Still
we are empty.

We want meaning.
We want stillness.
We want to set the lists down,
look into each other's eyes,
and stay.

We want to know
it isn't all for nothing.
That we matter.
That someone cares.
That we're worthy
not for what we produce,
but for simply being here.

We want more
than trauma masked by pills,
than fear dressed as normalcy.
We want to heal.
We want to dance.
We want to feel.

We want to cry
without shame.
We want to stay
without masks.
We want to walk together
into a different kind of life.

We want something more.
And we know
deep in our bones
that we were made for it.

From the Fumes

So
who am I?
Where am I from?
What threads
weave this life
into being?

Have I shut too many doors,
cut too many ties
to the roots that once
held me?

Have I forgotten?
Did I ever know?

I am born
from ashes.

From carbon monoxide fumes
that filled the garage
like a final breath.

I did not live
his death
but I've dreamt it
a thousand times.

I can almost smell
the burning skin.
I can almost hear
my mother's tears
before they fell.

All I remember
are the goldfish crackers
I ate on the day of his funeral.

Looking for smiles
in their baked faces,
not knowing
what was lost
only that something
had changed.

So maybe
I am from that.
From the fumes
that shaped a woman
before she had a name.

Maybe I am from bruises
carried in my mother's heart
from a love that hurt.

Or maybe I'm from
the moment
two sorrow-filled eyes
met
and chose joy anyway.

Maybe I am from
both.

Darkness
and the spark
that burns through it.

I look in the mirror
and don't always
recognize
the reflection.

There's a ringing
in my left ear
an alarm,
a calling,
or maybe
just the sound
of remembering.

I ask myself
Do I belong here?
Or am I made of somewhere else?

Smoke rolls in at midnight,
singing songs
of the parts of me
I try to hide.

Fog rises
and reveals
what I pretend
not to see.

I am not all darkness.
But I am not
all light.

The weight of pretending
lifts
when I say
I don't know who I am today.

And maybe that,
too,
is sacred.

Alchemy of Life

Writing this book of poetry
perhaps the bravest thing I've done.
It asked me to walk beside myself
and capture truth beneath the sun.

It brought me face to face with fire,
with embers I'd long left untold
it thawed the frost around my heart
and made the parts I buried bold.

It reconnected me to me,
to the magic in my name.
It asked me not to look away
but to step into the flame.

With a sensual hand I touched
the beauty pulsing in my days,
then turned to meet the shadows too
and kissed them with a gaze.

It called me down to the underworld
to gather what I'd lost,
to hold my pain with reverence,
no matter what it cost.

I sifted through old memories,
through grief I thought had died.
But poetry became the way
I let those ghosts inside.

I didn't fix, or rush, or judge
I let the tears just flow.
And somewhere in that sacred mess
I watched the healing grow.

I wove my voices all together
the girl I was, the one I've been,
the woman here who speaks aloud
the things I kept within.

And in the stitching of these words,
I found a truth that's mine:
The past was not a prison
it was a spark in my design.

This book became a mirror,
a ritual, a flame.
A story told in many keys,
yet singing one true name.

It's how I turned the ache to art,
the wounds to sacred gold.
It's how I met my life again,
and held it—soft and bold.

So may you meet your shadows too,
and feel them start to shift.

May you find that pain
is not the end
but the beginning
of your gift.

This is the work,
the way,
the light.

This is the Alchemy
of Life.